DISCOVERING GEOGRAPHY

POLLUTION AND CONSERVATION

Rebecca Hunter

www.raintreepublishers.co.uk
Visit our website to find out more information about **Raintree** books.

To order:
☎ Phone 44 (0) 1865 888112
📄 Send a fax to 44 (0) 1865 314091
💻 Visit the Raintree Bookshop at **www.raintreepublishers.co.uk** to browse our catalogue and order online.

First published in Great Britain by Raintree,
Halley Court, Jordan Hill, Oxford
OX2 8EJ, part of Harcourt Education.

Raintree is a registered trademark of Harcourt Education Ltd.

Produced for Raintree by Discovery Books Ltd
Design: Ian Winton
Editorial: Rebecca Hunter
Consultant: Jeremy Bloomfield
Commissioned photography: Chris Fairclough
Illustrations: Keith Williams, Stefan Chabluk and Pamela Goodchild
Production: Jonathan Smith

Originated by Dot Gradations Ltd
Printed and bound in China by South China Printing Company

ISBN 1 844 21679 9
07 06 05 04 03
10 9 8 7 6 5 4 3 2 1

British Library Cataloguing in Publication Data
Hunter, Rebecca
Pollution and Conservation. – (Discovering Geography)
363.7'3
A full catalogue record for this book is available from the British Library.

Acknowledgements
The publishers would like to thank the following for permission to reproduce photographs:
Bruce Coleman pp. **4** (John Shaw), **9** top (M.P.L Fogden), **11**, **21** top, **24** (Hans Reinhard), **27** top (Stafan Widstrands), bottom (Christer Fredriksson); Corbis pp. **10** bottom; Discovery Picture Library pp. **28** bottom; Getty Images pp. **5**, top and **7** (David Woodfall), **8** (Paul Edmondson), **10** top (Robert Frerck), **12** (Nick Vedros), **14** (Hans Peter Merten), **15** (Jeremy Walker), **21** bottom (Johnny Johnson), **26** (Tony Dawson); Oxford Scientific Films pp. **5** bottom (Mark Hamblin), **9** bottom (Scott Camazine), **18** (Richard Herrmann), **19** top (Ian West), **23** bottom (Kjell-Arne Larsson), **25** top (Martyn Colbeck), bottom (Kjell Sandved), **28** top (Chris Catton); Science Photo Library pp. **16** (Conor Caffrey), **19** bottom (Vanessa Vick), **22** and **23** top (Simon Fraser).

Cover photograph of beach polluted with rubbish reproduced with permission of Getty Images (Peter Cade).

The publishers would like to thank the following schools for their help in providing equipment, models and locations for photography sessions: Bedstone College, Bucknell, Moor Park, Ludlow and Packwood Haugh, Shrewsbury.

Every effort has been made to contact copyright holders of any material reproduced in this book.
Any omissions will be rectified in subsequent printings if notice is given to the publishers.

Any words appearing in the text in bold, **like this**, are explained in the Glossary.

CONTENTS

OUR ENVIRONMENT

Earth is our home. It is the only planet known to support life. It provides the food, water and air that living things need to survive. It also provides the energy and other natural resources that humans use. All of these parts of a living thing's surroundings make up the **environment**.

There are three main parts of the environment: the land, the water and the **atmosphere**. Plants, animals and humans live in and use all these parts of the environment.

Conservationists work hard to preserve the environment so that beautiful places like the Rocky Mountains, USA, survive.

Each living thing is adapted, or suited, to life in its environment. If its environment changes, the living thing must also change, or it will die. Many changes that take place in an environment are caused by nature. An erupting volcano can quickly burn away all the plants in an area, destroying the environment for many years.

Pollution from factories has killed these trees.

Animals can also change an environment. A beaver will dam a stream to make a pond. The pond creates homes for some animals while destroying the riverbanks where other animals and plants live.

Many changes in the environment are caused by humans. Some of these changes are for the better, but many cause great damage.

Old fishing nets are a danger to animals like this seal.

GIVE AND TAKE

We take many things from our planet. Trees are cut down to clear the land and to make buildings, furniture and paper. Fuels like coal, oil and natural gas are taken from under the ground.

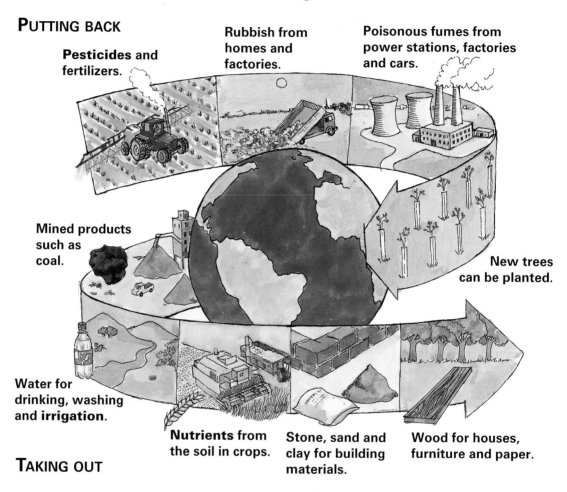

PUTTING BACK

Pesticides and fertilizers.

Rubbish from homes and factories.

Poisonous fumes from power stations, factories and cars.

Mined products such as coal.

New trees can be planted.

Water for drinking, washing and **irrigation**.

Nutrients from the soil in crops.

Stone, sand and clay for building materials.

Wood for houses, furniture and paper.

TAKING OUT

We put things back into the planet, too. Sadly the things we put back are often harmful things. Factories create many poisonous waste products that go into the air, rivers and oceans. Farmers and gardeners use insect-killing chemicals and **fertilizers** that rain carries into rivers. We create huge amounts of rubbish every day, so we must find a safe way to get rid of it.

POLLUTION AND CONSERVATION

Anything we put back into the **environment** that harms it or makes it dirty is called pollution. We are polluting Earth more and more every year.

Today there are more than 6 billion people in the world. This number is going to get bigger. The more people there are, the more damage is done to the world. We need to find ways to look after our planet and all our natural resources more carefully. This is called conservation.

DAMAGING THE LAND

The number of people in the world grows every day. This increase in people means we need more and more food to feed them. Farmers all over the world are looking for ways to produce more food. Many of these new methods harm the **environment**.

LOSS OF FORESTS

All over the world, forests have been chopped down to make room for farms. Northern Europe once had some of the largest forests in the world. Now nearly all of these have been cut down and replaced by fields and towns.

A tropical rainforest in Brazil after it was burned.

Today, the areas where most trees are being destroyed are the tropical rainforests. These forests grow in places where the **climate** is hot and wet all year. Rainforest trees, such as teak and mahogany, provide very beautiful wood. People use this wood to make furniture.

WAIT A MINUTE!
About 60 hectares of rainforest are cut down every minute. At this rate, there will be no rainforests left in 100 years.

Rainforests have more types of animal and plant **species** than any other environment on Earth. A species is the name we give to one particular type of animal or plant. As trees are cleared, many animals and birds lose their homes. When all the members of a species die, the species becomes **extinct**. At least 100 species of rainforest plants and animals are becoming extinct every day.

The golden toad from Costa Rica is now extinct in the wild.

RAINFOREST MEDICINES

Many medicines have been made from the plants in rainforests. Doctors use these to treat serious diseases, such as **malaria** and **cancer**. Scientists are discovering medicines made from plants all the time. It would be terrible if some special plants became extinct before we discovered how they might help us.

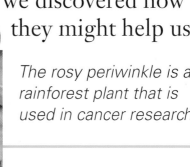

The rosy periwinkle is a rainforest plant that is used in cancer research.

SOIL EROSION

The leaves and roots of plants protect soil. They stop soil **erosion**. Erosion is when wind or rain blows or washes away soil. This soil ends up in rivers and lakes and is carried to the ocean. When too many animals feed on one area of land, the ground becomes bare of plants. This is called overgrazing. It can lead to soil erosion. Most plants cannot grow without soil. When the soil is lost, we cannot easily replace it.

◀ *This picture shows how soil has washed away after overgrazing in Mexico.*

Other harmful ways of farming can also cause erosion. In the USA in the 1930s, large dust storms blew away huge clouds of soil.

A dust storm in Colorado, USA, in 1935.

PROJECT

See how plant roots prevent erosion.

You will need:
two seed trays
some soil
grass seed
a watering can.

1. Fill both trays with soil. Plant one tray with grass seed.

2. Keep both trays damp and wait for the seeds to sprout.

3. Wait for the grass to grow to about 5 cm long. (This will take 2–3 weeks.)

4. Put both trays on a slope, and water with the watering can.

What happens to the soil in each tray?

The soil in the tray with the grass is held in place by plant roots. The soil in the other tray will be washed away by the water.

Soil erosion on hillsides can be stopped by cutting flat steps, or terraces, like these in Bali, Indonesia.

11

RUBBISH

This is how much rubbish the average person creates in a year:

ten times your weight in other products

90 drink cans

70 food cans

the paper from two trees

45 kilograms of plastics

110 bottles and jars

Have you ever thought where all this rubbish goes? Many things can be recycled. Paper, plastic, metal and glass can all be collected and made into new products. A large amount of rubbish is buried in huge holes in the ground. These are called landfills.

PROJECT

Look at the amount of glass, plastic and paper in a bag of shopping.

You will need:

a typical bag of shopping, for example:

a box of cereal

a packet of biscuits

6 cans of drink

a box of eggs

a bottle of soft drink

a box of washing powder.

Use these products, but keep the containers, boxes and packaging and do the following:

1. Weigh the containers. Do they weigh more than the contents?

2. Divide the containers into glass, metal, plastic and paper.

3. How much packaging can be recycled? How much do you have to throw away?

There are 4000 licenced landfill sites in the UK – but we are running out of places to make landfills. We need to find other ways to get rid of rubbish.

LIGHT FROM LITTER?

Over 75 landfill sites in the UK are generating electricity by burning the gases produced by rubbish.

INDUSTRIAL POLLUTION

Today we have many power stations, factories and machines that pollute the environment. We cannot do without the energy and goods that power stations and factories create, but we can try and make the processes cleaner.

Mining does a lot of damage to the environment. At an opencast mine, the top layer of soil is stripped away to reach the useful rocks that contain minerals or fuel.

This is an opencast coal mine in the UK.

Some companies leave huge piles of waste that cover large areas of land near the mines and factories. These places can be cleaned up. If the area is covered with soil, conservation groups can plant trees and other plants and make the area ready for use by humans or animals.

LIQUID WASTE

Factories often produce many liquid waste chemicals while they make their products. Sometimes this dangerous waste is piped into the **sewers**. **Treated** sewage can be used as **fertilizers** for crops. If the chemicals from the sewage remain in the fertilizers they could be harmful to the crops. People and animals who eat the crops could be poisoned.

Some factories pour their liquid waste directly into nearby rivers.

AIR AND WATER POLLUTION

Factories, power stations, cars, lorries and buses send smoke and gases into the air. These pollute the **atmosphere**. Air pollution causes at least 150,000 deaths worldwide each year.

Air pollution in Mexico City.

Today, the amount of smoke in the atmosphere has been reduced – but the number of other polluting gases has increased. Big industrial cities often have a layer of pollution hanging over them. In Mexico City, the air pollution is so thick that drivers often have to turn their lights on in the middle of the day.

PROJECT

Measure air pollution.

You will need:
a jar
a funnel
some filter paper or kitchen roll
a magnifying glass
a rainy day.

1. Line the funnel with the filter paper and place it in the jar.

2. Leave the jar outside in the rain for at least 30 minutes.

3. Bring it in and let the filter paper dry out.

4. Examine anything that has collected on the filter paper with a magnifying glass. Can you see the tiny pieces of dirt that have been washed out by the rain?

You can try this experiment in different places: a city centre, a town, a park, the countryside. Which place has the dirtiest air?

OZONE

The atmosphere is the layer of gases that surrounds Earth. One of these gases is ozone. A layer of ozone in the upper atmosphere helps block out the Sun's harmful rays. Spray cans, fire extinguishers and refrigerators can all contain chemicals that destroy the ozone layer.

There are now huge holes in the ozone layer above Antarctica and the Arctic. If these holes are allowed to get bigger, we will all be in danger from rays that can cause skin **cancer**.

WATER POLLUTION

Water is one of the most common substances on Earth. Life would be impossible without water. Even so, many of our water sources, including the oceans, are being slowly poisoned.

One of the biggest polluters of the ocean is sewage. Sewage should be **treated** before it reaches rivers or the oceans, but often it is not. If **raw sewage** gets into drinking water, many people become seriously ill.

Many beaches around the world are now so dirty they are unsafe for swimming.

OIL POLLUTION

Oil tankers sometimes run aground, spilling their cargo. Thousands of tonnes of oil can be spilled into the water in hours. The thick, black oil floats on the surface of the water. An oil spill can kill millions of ocean animals. Oil sticks to the feathers of seabirds. Then they cannot fly. If they try to clean themselves, they swallow oil that will poison them. Most oil-soaked birds die from cold or starvation.

▲ Rescue groups try to catch and clean seabirds caught in oil spills, but it is usually too late for most of them.

In 1989 the oil tanker Exxon Valdez hit a reef in Alaska's Prince William Sound. It spilled 42 million litres of oil.

WORLD PROBLEMS

The world's **climates** are always changing. At certain times in the past, the world was much warmer than it is today. At other times, it was much colder, and ice covered huge areas of Earth. Climates change naturally, but many scientists believe that the climate today is being changed by humans.

THE GREENHOUSE EFFECT

The gases in Earth's **atmosphere** work like a greenhouse. They trap the Sun's heat and warm Earth. This is called the 'greenhouse effect', and it makes our planet warm enough to live on. However, today we are producing too many of the gases that trap heat, which would otherwise escape into space. This may be causing the temperatures on Earth to rise.

Sun's rays

some heat escapes

some heat is trapped

The greenhouse effect.

You might think it would be nice to live in a warmer world – but it would not just mean better weather. As temperatures rise, ice at the North and South Poles will melt, and the sea level will rise. Many towns and cities on the coasts will be flooded.

▲ *The Maldives are a group of low-lying islands. A small rise in sea level would flood them completely.*

Polar habitats will be the first to change as the world warms up. Ice sheets will melt and animals such as polar bears will lose their home and hunting ground.

Global warming will also cause other problems. Some areas will become hotter and drier, and some much wetter. These areas will suffer more from **droughts** and floods. It may become impossible for people to live there. As land is lost under the ocean, more people will be squeezed on to less land. We must stop polluting the atmosphere to slow down global warming.

ACID RAIN

Chemicals set free into the atmosphere by factories, power stations and cars can pollute the rain as well as the air. This polluted rain is called **acid rain**.

These trees were killed by acid rain.

Acid rain is poisonous to plants and can strip trees of their leaves. Whole forests can be destroyed. When acid rain reaches rivers and lakes, the plants and animals that live there begin to die. Acid rain is worst in areas with many industries, such as northern Europe and the north-eastern USA.

Acid rain does not just affect plants and animals. The stonework of buildings and statues is often damaged by it. It seeps into our water supplies and drinking water, making us ill.

▶ *The Church of St. Peter and St. Paul in Cracow, Poland, has been damaged by acid rain and air pollution.*

To reduce acid rain, we need to cut down on the amount of chemicals released into the air. The burning of fuels, like coal and oil, is one of the main causes of acid rain. We should try to find cleaner energy sources that do not release chemicals into the atmosphere. We can also help by using our cars less.

This helicopter is spreading a chemical called lime over a forest to combat acid rain pollution in Sweden.

WILDLIFE IN DANGER

The rate at which animals and plants are becoming **extinct** is now higher than ever before. Hundreds of **species** die out every day. Extinctions have always happened naturally on Earth. Often they are caused by a change in **climate**. This is probably why the dinosaurs died out 65 million years ago.

HABITAT DESTRUCTION

Today the main cause of extinction is humans. Thousands of animals and plants are in danger because the places where they live are being destroyed. Forests are cut down and wetlands are drained to farm or build on the land. The **environment** is changed so much that animals and plants cannot survive.

The destruction of the Chinese bamboo forests means there are less than 1000 giant pandas left in the wild.

HUNTING

Hunting is another danger to wildlife. People hunt animals for food and for their fur, hide and horns. Sometimes they hunt just for fun.

African elephants are killed for their tusks. They are a protected species, but are still being killed by poachers.

Sometimes other animals are put in danger by careless fishing methods. The fishing nets that are used to catch tuna often catch dolphins, too. Many people stopped buying cans of tuna until the fishing companies agreed to change their methods.

PLANTS IN DANGER

Many plants are also at risk from humans. Colourful flowers are used to make dyes for materials. Many orchids are in danger because people dig them up from the wild.

The largest flower in the world is almost extinct in the wild in Sumatra, Indonesia.

CONSERVATION

People all over the world are trying to stop pollution and the destruction of forests. Conservation and wildlife groups are calling on governments, businesses and individual people to help with global conservation. Here are some of the actions that governments are taking.

The government of British Columbia, Canada, has set aside over 4 million hectares of land for the protection of animals. These animals include caribou, grizzly bears, wolves and buffalo.

Denmark will build 500 offshore wind power stations in a cleaner energy programme. This will help reduce pollution caused by power stations burning coal or oil.

New conservation laws will protect the Galápagos Islands in the Pacific from damage by tourism and development. These laws will help safeguard giant tortoises (right) and other **species** found only in the Galápagos.

Nepal has declared Kanchenjunga (below), the world's third highest mountain, a special conservation area. This region is home to red pandas, snow leopards and more than 25,000 species of flowering plants. These conservation projects are helping to solve some of the environmental problems that our planet faces.

WHAT CAN YOU DO?

There are many ways in which we could make our planet cleaner and safer to live on. Each one of us can do a lot to clean up our own **environment**. Don't leave litter lying around. All forms of rubbish are dangerous to wildlife.

◄ *This duck is caught in the plastic rings that hold drink cans together.*

RECYCLING

Most towns and cities now have recycling centres. Glass, cans, paper and some plastics can all be recycled again and again. Buying goods that are made out of recycled materials is a good idea. It will encourage more industries to make them.

SAVING ENERGY

Persuade your family to use the car less. Walk or ride your bike when you can. Save energy in the house by turning off lights or machines when they are not being used.

PROJECT

Make recycled paper.

You will need:

some waste paper (newspaper, tissue, and drawing paper are all good to use)
a food blender, or mixer
water
a large bowl
some food colouring
a thin piece of old material
an old picture frame
some drawing pins
an adult to help.

1. Tear up your waste paper and leave it to soak in water overnight.

2. Ask your adult to help you make paper pulp by liquidizing the soaked waste paper.

3. Fill a large bowl with paper pulp and add a few drops of food colouring if you want to make your paper coloured. Stir up the pulp. It should be as thick as cream. Add more water if necessary.

4. Tack the material over the picture frame tightly, using the drawing pins.

5. Dip the frame in the paper pulp until it is under the surface. Turn the frame flat in the bowl and pull it out slowly. The water will drain away leaving a covering of pulp on the net.

6. Leave the frame outside to dry.

7. When the paper is totally dry, you will be able to peel it off the frame.

GLOSSARY

acid rain rain that has become acidic because of pollution in the air

atmosphere layer of gases that surrounds Earth

cancer disease causing lumps called tumours in the body. Often it cannot be cured.

climate usual weather in one place during the seasons and from one year to another

drought long period with no rain

environment area that an animal or plant lives in

erosion wearing away of Earth's surface by water, wind or ice

extinct when all the members of a species have died out

fertilizer chemical that is put on the land to make crops grow well

irrigate to supply land or crops with water

malaria tropical disease that causes fevers

mining process of getting minerals or fuels (for example, coal) out of the ground

nutrient substance in food that plants and animals use for growth

pesticide chemical that is sprayed on plants to kill pests such as insects

raw sewage waste from toilets and drains

sewers drains that carry away waste or sewage

species type or kind of animal or plant

treated (sewage) processed to make cleaner

FURTHER INFORMATION

BOOKS

Atlas of Endangered Resources, Steve Pollock (Belitha Press, 1995)

Endangered Species, Mike Unwin (Franklin Watts, 2000)

Energy for life: Energy Alternatives, Robert Snedden (Heinemann Library, 2001)

Ocean Watch: The young person's guide to protecting the planet, Martyn Bramwell (Dorling Kindersley, 2001)

Waste, Recycling and Reuse: Our Impact on the Planet, Rob Bowden (Hodder Wayland, 2001)

Wildlife in Danger, Sally Morgan (Franklin Watts, 2002)

WEBSITES

Conservation Breeding Specialist Group – This group helps protect threatened plants and animals. Explore the global zoo directory.
http://www.cbsg.org

Conservation International – find out where they operate, read their news, check out their online library, and find out how to help.
http://www.conservation.org

EduGreen – have fun while you learn about the environment! Read about life on Earth, air pollution, climate change, water and more. You can also play games, try out activities, and read stories!
http://edugreen.teri.res.in

Future Forests – organization in the UK promoting tree planting to offset carbon dioxide emissions. Learn a lot about this pollution problem with their interactive Flash presentations too!
http://www.futureforests.com

INDEX

Titles in the Discovering Geography series include:

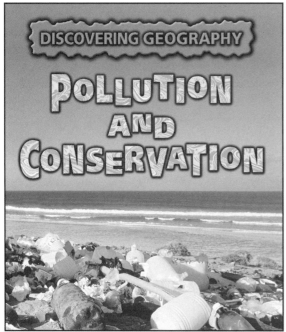

Hardback   1 844 21679 9

Hardback   1 844 21680 2

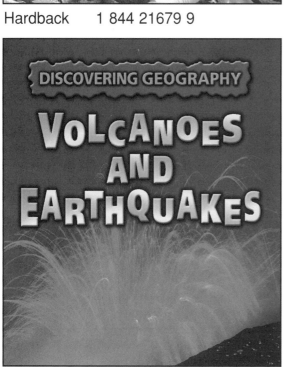

Hardback   1 844 21681 0

Hardback   1 844 21682 9

Find out about the other titles in this series on our website www.raintreepublishers.co.uk